Growing Grace

Erin Mason
Illustrated by Layal Idriss

Copyright © 2020 by Erin Mason.
Second Edition.
All rights reserved to Erin Mason.

No part of this book may be reproduced in any form
without written permission from the publisher.

ISBN: 978-0-9991271-1-7

Illustrated by Layal Idriss
Design by Hala Buhnaq

*To Amanda with all my love... Now and always.
And for my mom who taught me what love means.*

A girl...

Almost a grown-up, but not quite...
Discovered she was going to have a baby.

Still being a young girl herself,
she knew nothing about raising a baby.

She hadn't done any of the things,
she was supposed to do yet.

She hadn't finished school.
She didn't have a job.

She didn't even know what she wanted to be
when she grew up.

The girl understood being a mother was a very big, and important responsibility.

She was scared, and didn't know what to do.

The longer she thought, the more the baby grew inside her belly.

As the baby grew, a special light inside the girl's heart also began to grow.

With the light in her heart,
somehow the girl already knew the baby inside.

She knew how the baby would look.
She knew what the baby would like to do.
She knew what the baby would want.

And the girl worried that she wouldn't be
able to give the baby all it needed.

After all, she was still a young girl.

By the time the snow started to fall that year,
the girl found out her baby was a girl too.

She named the baby girl growing inside her, Grace.

Like a flame, the light in the girl's heart began to glow.

She took care of Grace the best she knew how.

The girl rubbed her growing belly so
Grace would know she was protected.

She told stories to Grace,
and sang songs to her at bedtime.

She ate healthy foods like fresh fruit and oatmeal
muffins, and only had milkshakes *sometimes*.

But most importantly, the girl told Grace
over and over how much she loved her.

Every time she said it,
the light in her heart grew more vibrant.

Sometimes she whispered her love.
Sometimes she shouted it out loud.
Sometimes she said it in her dreams.
Sometimes her love came with tears.
Still, the light became brighter.

As the baby inside her grew bigger,
the girl realized she only had a little
time left to spend with her.

And so she began to search for the
perfect parents to raise Grace.

She searched in the mountains,
where the people were strong, and kind.

Their town was cold and they wore
thick coats almost all year long.

She searched near the ocean,
where the people were calm, and happy.

Their beach was wide, and sometimes the
wind would blow very strongly and the waves
would wash big shells and stones to the shore.

She searched in the city,
where the people were excited, and friendly.

Their city was very busy,
and everyone moved so fast.

She could only walk with them
if she ran to catch up.

The girl became tired, and weary as
she searched for the right parents for Grace.

Still, the light in her heart was strong.

Then one day she received a letter in the mail from a couple who lived in a valley.

The couple said that more than anything in the world, they wanted to have a baby to love.

The girl went to visit the couple in the valley.

The valley was green, and full of sunshine with white,
puffy clouds in the day,
and thousands of glittering stars at night.

The couple was full of love,
and they wanted to understand all the things
the girl already knew about the baby growing inside her.

She could see in their eyes how much they already loved the baby.

Although, the couple couldn't see the light in the girl's heart, they could feel its warmth and knew how much the girl also loved baby Grace.

When the snow began to melt,
and the first yellow daffodil peeked around the corner,
the girl made a promise.

She made a promise to Grace that she would always love her and
never forget the wonderful months they shared,
while Grace grew inside her tummy.

And she promised the couple they could raise little Grace,
and help her become a grown-up.

This was an extremely difficult promise and made the girl very sad.

The girl loved Grace so much, she did not want to let her go.

The light in her heart began to flicker but never went out.

Still, it *glowed*.

The time came for the baby to enter the world.

From the first moment,
the girl could see that Grace also held a light
inside her heart.

For three beautiful days, the girl held Grace.

She held her as close as she could.

She fed her, tickled her tiny feet,
and kissed her rosy lips.

Until the day when the girl had to fulfill her promise.

The bright light in her heart began to ache and burn.

With tears in her eyes, the girl said goodbye to the baby... who had grown inside her.

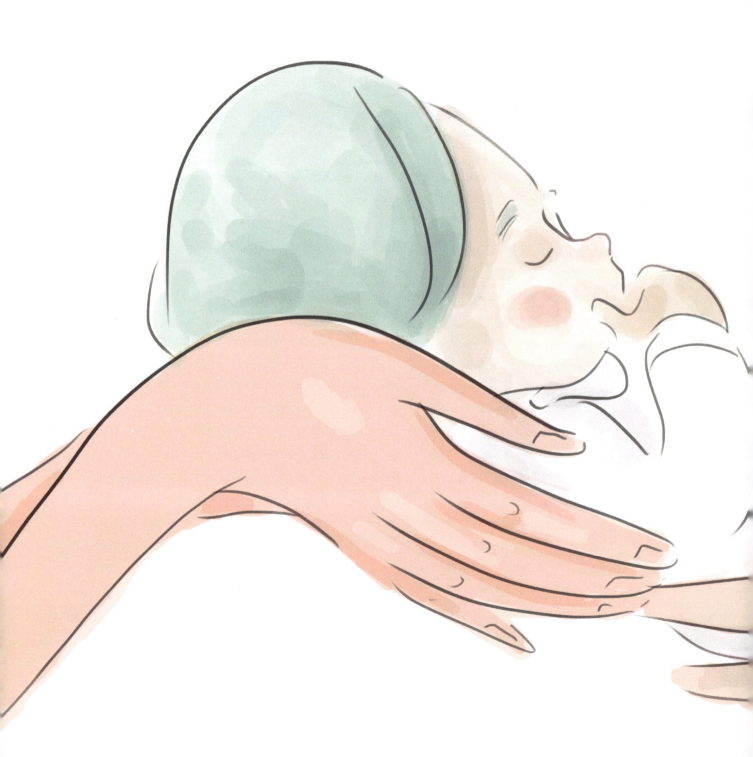

She placed Grace carefully in the arms of the couple, and closed her eyes as they walked away toward their home in the green valley.

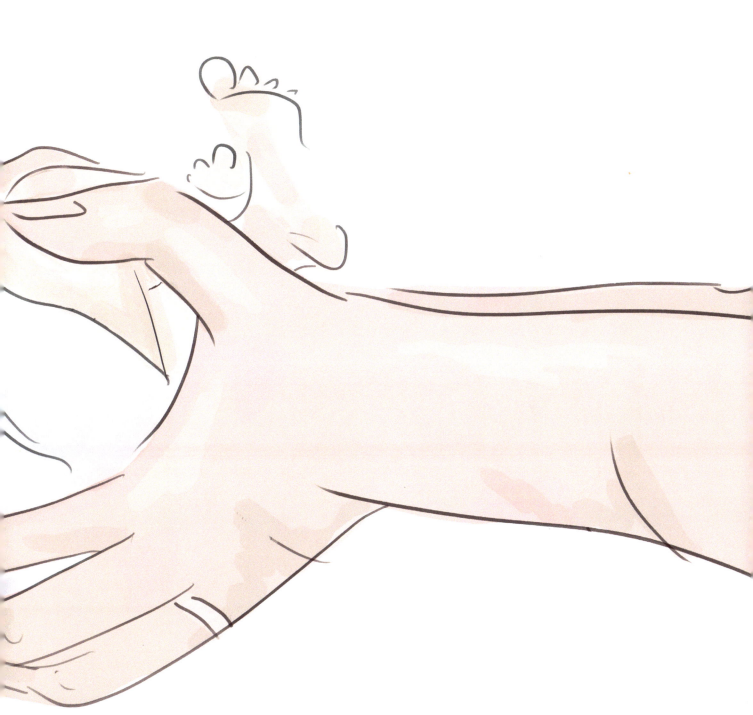

The girl knew the valley wouldn't always have sunshine, and white puffy clouds in the day and thousands of glittering stars at night.

But, the girl did know that the couple would always love Grace, and take very good care of her.

The years passed by, but the girl never stopped missing Grace.

She still holds the light in her heart,
and always remembers the baby she carried inside.

Sometimes she rubs her belly to feel Grace's presence,
or whispers how much she loves her, and hopes she can be
heard far away in the green valley.

As Grace grows up, her light will shine brightly
in its own unique way.

The girl doesn't know if,
or when they will meet again.

But, she believes the light Grace created will
live inside each of them,
and will continue to connect them...

Now, and always.

Erin Mason the Author

A licensed psychotherapist in Los Angeles, Erin began her career 20 years ago at a residential facility for pregnant and parenting teens.

Now in private practice, she is continuously inspired by her clients' resiliency, determination, and quest for self-understanding.

Over the years, Erin has discovered that once the conversation is initiated, many people have either had a direct relationship with adoption or know someone who has been impacted by the experience.

Intimately affected by adoption herself, and with tremendous respect and appreciation for all parties involved, Erin sheds a fresh perspective on the adoption experience.

Growing Grace

Conversation Starters for Parents and Kids

Children are often better able to understand and engage in conversation while reading a book or looking at/drawing pictures.

Consider how each child may be at different levels of comprehension, depending on age, cognitive development and their own unique adoption story.

Thank you for being part of the journey

General Adoption Questions

- What does adoption mean?
- Do you have questions about your adoption? You know it's okay to ask, right?
- What is a mom/dad? What is a "birth mom/dad?" What's similar or different?
- What do you know of or imagine about your birth mom/dad?
  (share facts or let your child use his/her imagination)
- Can you draw a picture of what you think your birth mom/dad looks like?
- Do you ever think of your birth family?
- Do you wonder if your birth family is thinking about you?
- Do you ever get sad that you aren't living with your birth mom/dad or wonder why you were adopted? Do you wonder if you birth mom/dad loves you?
- Do you ever wonder if you have any brothers or sisters?
- Do you wonder if you will get to meet your birth mom/dad/siblings?

Growing Grace Questions

- Why couldn't "the girl" take care of the baby?
- What does it mean to be a grown-up?
- What do you want to be when you grow up?
- What is a parent's job? What kind of responsibilities do parents have?
- What is that light inside of the girl?
- What does the light mean? Love? Hope? Connection?
  (the birth mom, adoptive family, and the child all have different kinds of light)
- What color is your light? What do you think your light means?
- How do you think the girl feels?
- What do you do when you feel scared/sad/worried/happy/confused?
- What was the girl searching/looking for?
- What does it mean to make a promise?
- What does it feel like to say goodbye to someone you love very much?
- How do you think the couple felt when the baby was placed in their arms?
  How did we (your parents) feel when you were placed in our arms?

Printed in the USA
CPSIA information can be obtained
at www.ICGtesting.com
LVHW071043131023
760813LV00022B/1216